THE TRUTH BEGINS WITH YOU

CBC continues
to be with
you in spirit

Claudette Black

THE
TRUTH
Begins
WITH YOU

....

CLAUDIA BLACK, PhD

Illustrations by Lynne Adamson

Reflections to Heal Your Spirit

CENTRAL RECOVERY PRESS

CENTRAL RECOVERY PRESS

Central Recovery Press (CRP) is committed to publishing exceptional materials addressing addiction treatment, recovery, and behavioral health care topics, including original and quality books, audio/visual communications, and web-based new media. Through a diverse selection of titles, we seek to contribute a broad range of unique resources for professionals, recovering individuals and their families, and the general public.

For more information, visit www.centralrecoverypress.com.
Central Recovery Press, Las Vegas, NV 89129

Publisher: Central Recovery Press
           3321 N. Buffalo Drive
           Las Vegas, NV 89129

22 21 20 19 18 17   2 3 4 5

ISBN-13: 978-1-936290-61-1 (paper)
ISBN-10: 1-936290-61-8

Cover design and illustrations by Lynne Adamson
Interior design and layout by Sara Streifel, Think Creative Design

In memory of

Earnie Larsen and Father Joseph Martin,

two of my heroes, healers whose words

and love continue to offer inspiration

and hope to millions.

Introduction

As a child I was said to have been very quiet and polite, a little girl with long braids and of few words. Growing up with a lot of confusion about why things happened as they did, I was ever so vigilant, listening and watching. Like many in similar situations, I ventured forth with pragmatism about survivorship—introspective—believing that no one deserves to live a life of fear. Not me, not you. As a young girl, I was developing clarity within a belief system that would drive me in my professional work and personal life. I am not sure I understood the process as it was occurring, but in hindsight I realize that I ultimately "stood tall in the face of my truths." In my healing process, I began to offer to others what I also needed to hear: "Your strengths are more powerful than your vulnerabilities." "You are very special. You may never have had the opportunity to believe in your specialness. You may believe in it today."

As is true for all of us, I have had many life lessons and with those lessons I continue to listen to what has given me strength. I try to live my life "walking the walk," hoping to make a difference in people's lives by speaking to their hearts with words that offer love and connection. I have worked with thousands of people who have struggled for various reasons; people challenged with losses and addiction, who are angry, lost and confused, and simply afraid. Whatever the complexity of your life experience, these short statements are meant to support you in being true to yourself, valuing yourself, and celebrating your preciousness.

Use this book in whatever way supports you at any given time. It may become a part of your morning or bedtime ritual. Perhaps you'll carry it with you or keep it close by in your purse, on your desk, or in your car. You never know when you might need a moment of grounding or inspiration. I hope its pages become dog-eared, as you mark the favorites that you go back to time and time again. I can also envision the sayings offering a source for conversation among friends and family. At the back, you will find a few blank pages to note thoughts or sayings that you want to add for yourself.

My wish for you is that you find comfort, inspiration, and hope in these thoughts in a way that ultimately translates into actions that support a life of self-care, self-love, and integrity. Remember, "The truth begins with you—your truth."

The truth
begins with you—
your truth.

There is a path out of
any painful situation.

*Your strengths
are more powerful than
your vulnerabilities.*

You are perfect
in your imperfections.

It is in acceptance
of all that was and is
that your spirit
becomes whole.

The goal of healing is
not to let go of feelings,
but to no longer
allow them to dictate
how you live your life.

In many languages
the word spirit means
breath or to breathe.
Stop. Take a breath.

Know yourself;
it will be the gift that you
offer in sharing yourself
with another.

Intimacy is touch
and being touched in heart,
mind, body, and soul.

Feelings are to be
listened to—they are
the cues and signals
telling you what you need.

The greater your inner
strength and ability
to trust in yourself,
the more willing you are
to take risks.

Boundaries empower
you to determine
how you'll be treated
by others.

You have the right
to say "no."
When you say "no"
you are actually saying
"yes" to yourself.

It's time to break
the dysfunctional
family rules of
"don't talk, don't feel,
don't trust."

A healthy relationship
is about the sharing of
strengths and autonomy;
it is not about control.

Healthy communication
is listening with
honor and speaking
with respect.

In faith, you find
strength to survive
times of great fear
and sadness.

Healing takes time;
it is a process,
not an event.

You can't be honest in the here and now when you continue to deny your childhood experiences.

Becoming whole
involves the journey into
and through the
wounds of childhood.

Once upon a time
you were a child. May
the child in your heart
remain forever free.

Feelings are from
your heart and
what your heart
wants to tell you.

You deserve
to live your life
free of fear,
denial, and shame.

Resiliency means
putting one foot in front
of the other with both
courage and trust in the
face of adversity.

Embrace both
your masculine and
feminine strengths.

Meditation offers the
opportunity to clear
your mind and to
be present with the
here and now.

Recovery isn't
changing who you are.
It is letting go of
who you are not.

Learning to love yourself
does not mean you
love others less;
it frees you to
love them more.

You often live in the extremes—the "all or nothing," the numbers one or ten. Finding balance means learning the word "some"— living between the numbers two through nine.

Your needs are important.
Knowing your needs
is the first step in
getting them met.

Your best decisions
and choices come from
a place of inner knowing
and integrity.

Once upon a time
you were a child. May
the child in your heart
remain forever free.

Feelings are from
your heart and
what your heart
wants to tell you.

You deserve
to live your life
free of fear,
denial, and shame.

Resiliency means
putting one foot in front
of the other with both
courage and trust in the
face of adversity.

Embrace both
your masculine and
feminine strengths.

Meditation offers the
opportunity to clear
your mind and to
be present with the
here and now.

Recovery isn't
changing who you are.
It is letting go of
who you are not.

Surround yourself
with people who
respect and
treat you well.

It is safe to take
time to play today.
Play fuels your creativity,
tickles your inner child,
and nurtures your soul.

Laughter ignites
a spark of joy.

Intimacy is trusting
another with who
you are without the
fear of rejection.

It doesn't matter
which spiritual path
you take, what's important
is that you keep moving
forward and growing on
the path you choose.

You are of
value irrespective
of mistakes
you may make.

Freedom is
surrendering the illusion
that you have
all the answers.

Say "I love you,"
and say it often.
"I love you" is a
complete sentence.

Believe in
your right to happiness,
dignity, and respect.

Asking for help
is an act of courage.
You are a
very brave soul.

Don't confuse your
loving feelings with
not being free to be
angry or not having a voice.
Anger does not have to
mean a lessening of love.

You may have many
feelings at the same time.
This does not mean you
are going crazy. It means
you are having many
feelings at the same time.

Your relationships
can only be as healthy
as you are.

Other people's behavior
is a statement about them,
not about your
worth and value.

You lose sight
of your true self
when you act out
in emotional pain.

Accept both
your power and
powerlessness in life.

You are the fulfiller
of your own life script.

Trust in yourself
and give voice
to your truth.

Addressing unfinished
grief allows you to
put the past behind you
and to be present
in your life today.

What has occurred
in your life is yours,
not to be negated by
anyone else's experience.

To begin healing,
you must stop pretending,
denying, minimizing,
and rationalizing.

While you cannot change the past, may you come to accept it, focusing on new possibilities that come with each day.

You will find strength
and freedom when you
are willing to walk
through the pain rather
than around it.

Keep your head
where your feet are—
in the present.

There may have been
times when you were your
own worst enemy; today
you have the choice to be
your own greatest champion.

The greatest act of
abandonment is the
abandonment of self.

Ultimately, it is your own powerful spirit that will heal you.

Trust in yourself.
Your perceptions are often
far more accurate than
you are willing to believe.

To rid yourself of shame, be willing to show yourself.

Being willing to believe
in yourself allows you to
take the next step forward.

You won't get to
a place of heartfelt
forgiveness without being
emotionally honest.

Success is not relative
to others; it is a feeling
of love and accomplishment
for yourself.

Your spirit acknowledges
and does homage to
the spark of
divinity within you.

Mistakes are a
sign of growing.
Remember, be gentle
with yourself.

Recognize and honor
what is unique about
you and your history.

The insight that comes in acknowledging your past and connecting that experience to today is vital to developing compassion for yourself.

You deserve to have
a healthy and nurturing
relationship with yourself.

As you let go of your
self-defeating thoughts
and behaviors—you are in a
position to act, not react.

You are not responsible
for others' behaviors,
thoughts, and feelings.
You are responsible
for yours.

Trust can be rebuilt;
it begins with
trusting yourself.

You only need to
live one day at a time.

Your fears are often
far greater than reality.

Assuming leads to
false realities.
Ask. Inquire.

When you speak your truth,
you are not betraying
those you love. When you
don't speak your truth,
you betray yourself.

You no longer need
to go through life in
"one up-one down"
relationships.

Today you have choices.

Recovery is learning
to tolerate your feelings
without the need
to engage in
self-defeating behaviors.

Recognizing that you are in the process of recovery, you begin to shine your own light.

Accept yourself for who
you are—no longer
waiting for others to
define or approve of you.

Stand tall in the
face of truth.
Trust your perceptions.
Give voice to your reality.

Any substance or behavior that interferes with the ability to be honest with yourself deserves your attention.

Denial allows you to
normalize behavior when
your gut tells you there
is something more.
Trust your instincts.

The shame-based belief
that "you are not okay"
is something learned from
the outside. You are born
inherently precious.

With every tear that
is shed and every cry
of anguish that is released,
the heart is opened
for healing.

Having healthy
boundaries is the ability
to discriminate with
whom and when and
what to share.

The key to separating
true guilt from false guilt
is recognizing where
responsibility lies.

May you find
a path that leads to
greater acceptance.

You are very special.
You may never have had
the opportunity to believe
in your specialness.
You may believe in it today.

When there is loss,
there are tears.
Tears are the
elixir of healing.

Forgiveness is the
peace you feel when
you stop trying to punish
those who hurt you.

Setting boundaries means
reclaiming the power you
have given away by taking
responsibility for yourself.

You deserve to live
a life unencumbered
by sexual stigma.

Letting go of secrets
can feel like the warmth
of a summer sun after
a long cold winter.

Being less than perfect
makes you human.

Slow down, take a deep breath, ask for guidance, and move forward. Slow down, then breathe again, ask for guidance, and move forward again. Slow down, then breathe again...

To free yourself
from the past, you must
break the rules of
silence and compliance.

Healthy boundaries
bring order to your life.

"No" and "yes" are parts
of the same continuum.
"No" and "yes" are choices.

Anger is a natural response
to loss. It is a protest;
an attempt to retrieve
what is gone or acquire
what never was.

Don't put "shoulds"
on yourself.

It's not about
doing it right or wrong;
it's about doing your best.

A healthy boundary
protects without isolating,
contains without
imprisoning.

You are not your pain.
What you do about your pain
is a choice you make.

Recovery is not a solitary journey; it is about connection with self and others.

In accepting your own limitations, you learn to accept the limitations of others.

The spiritual path
is a commitment to
personal transformation,
to service, and to
not harming others.

With a willingness
to change,
recovery is possible.

Life-changing
transformations
take courage.

The greater your
fear, the greater
the need to let
others offer support.

Connect with
and love your
extraordinary self.

Your healing journey
is a gift to yourself.

Respect is an attitude
for which courtesy
is an expression.

Listen to your inner
child not with criticism,
but with openness.
Love the child for all
he or she had to
defend against.

With trust comes
the opportunity for intimacy
with self and others.

Relationships
need time.

The people in your life
are like characters in a play.
Learn to not judge those
who move in and out,
but to honor them
when they appear.

Community is a place
of belonging and
connection—an
opportunity to come
together for support,
guidance, and celebration.

Spirituality is the
ability to accept and the
capacity to give love.

Recovery is about
creating change for yourself.
All else that comes is
an unexpected gift.

Forgiving is not forgetting.
It is remembering
and letting go.

Resentments deplete
your happiness.

True guilt is remorse
or regret for something
you have done or not
done. False guilt is taking
responsibility for someone
else's behaviors and actions.
Take responsibility
for what is yours.

Making amends requires
changing your behavior.

When you forgive,
you no longer need your
grudges and resentments,
your hatred, your self-pity.

Personal spirituality
is a blend of your intent
to be authentic
and openness to
your inner knowing.

Healthy relationships
have moments of closeness
and separation and
moments of intensity
and quiet.

Today you have
choices about whom
you invite in to
share your life.

You can't go forward
without owning the past.

You can let go
of childhood family
rules and roles when
you no longer operate
from fear and shame.

Faith is trusting
the process of letting go.

Recovery is not linear;
there will be
no straight lines.

May you choose
to live a life of
serenity and peace.

You are responsible
for how you
live your life.

Accept your body
and find strengths
in your physical
vulnerabilities.

You never again
have to walk through
the pain alone.

You can't live
your life by walking
someone else's path.

The fears of what
will happen if you express
your feelings are often
based in your childhood.
Today you can respond
with the vulnerability of
your child and with the
strength of your adult.

You set boundaries
to honor and
protect yourself,
not to punish another.

Secrets become
confidences when
shared with safe people.

Healing begins
when you allow yourself
the benefit of getting to
know others who have walked
the path before you and who
will now walk alongside you.

When you have faith
you give up the need to
control. Faith and control
cannot peacefully coexist.

Today you have
the opportunity to live
your life differently.

Extend the
courtesy of forgiveness
to yourself.

Hope inspires
and energizes,
illuminating
the possibilities.

Don't let your
inner critic sit on
your inner child.

Applaud your steps
in the healing journey;
it is not the mountain
that gets moved, but the little
steps along the way that
make the difference.

You are good enough!
You are good enough!
You are good enough!

Pause . . .

Your time to heal
has come.

MY TRUTHS

....

....

....

....

....

....

....

....

....

....

....

....

....

....

....

....

....

....

MY THOUGHTS

MY FAVORITE QUOTES

Acknowledgments

I want to express my gratitude for the many people in my life who support me, challenge me, and love me—they are a part of knowing that my truth begins with me. I would like to acknowledge those whose presence I felt in the time I worked on this book, and those who have been directly involved and have made this a fun and meaningful experience.

My thanks to:
Nancy Schenck, my editor, who moved this manuscript through its various stages, making it not just stress-free, but exciting. Together we read each word, often rereading the messages that spoke to both of us in our own journeys.

Sandi Klein, my assistant of many years, and Jack Fahey, my husband of even more years, who also joined me in the fine crafting of words that hopefully have created inspiring messages. To you, a hug and a kiss.

Mel Pohl, a dear friend, whose love and support have been nothing short of heartfelt and fun.

Stuart Smith and Bob Gray who realize that at times it is the brevity that makes the impact and saw the importance of such a book.

ALSO AVAILABLE FROM CENTRAL RECOVERY PRESS

www.centralrecoverypress.com

INSPIRATIONAL

Above and Beyond: 365 Meditations for Transcending Chronic Pain and Illness
J.S. Dorian • $15.95 US •
ISBN-13: 978-1-9362-9066-6

Guide Me in My Recovery: Prayers for Times of Joy and Times of Trial
Rev. John T. Farrell, Ph.D. • $12.95 US •
ISBN-13: 978-1-936290-00-0

Special hardcover gift edition: $19.95 US •
ISBN-13: 978-1-936290-02-4

The Soul Workout: Getting and Staying Spiritually Fit
Helen H. Moore • $12.95 US •
ISBN-13: 978-0-9799869-8-7

Tails of Recovery: Addicts and the Pets That Love Them
Nancy A. Schenck • $19.95 US •
ISBN-13: 978-0-9799869-6-3

Of Character: Building Assets in Recovery
Denise D. Crosson, Ph.D. • $12.95 US •
ISBN-13: 978-0-9799869-2-5

MEMOIRS

Riding a Straight and Twisty Road: Motorcycles, Recovery, and Personal Journeys
James Hesketh • $16.95 US •
ISBN-13: 978-1-936290-05-5

Dopefiend: A Father's Journey from Addiction to Redemption
Tim Elhajj • $16.95 US •
ISBN 13: 978-1-936290-63-5

Leave the Light On: A Memoir of Recovery and Self-Discovery
Jennifer Storm • $14.95 US •
ISBN-13: 978-0-9818482-2-8

The Mindful Addict: A Memoir of the
Awakening of a Spirit
Tom Catton • $18.95 US •
ISBN-13: 978-0-9818482-7-3

Becoming Normal: An Ever-Changing Perspective
Mark Edick • $14.95 US •
ISBN-13: 978-0-9818482-1-1

RELATIONSHIPS

Disentangle: When You've Lost Your Self in
Someone Else
Nancy L. Johnston, MS, LPC, LSATP •
$15.95 US • ISBN-13: 978-1-936290-03-1

A Spiritual Path to a Healthy Relationship:
A Practical Approach
Steve McCord, MFT and Angie McCord, CC •
$15.95 US • ISBN-13: 978-1-936290-65-9

From Heartbreak to Heart's Desire: Developing
a Healthy GPS (Guy Picking System)
Dawn Maslar, MS • $14.95 US •
ISBN-13: 978-0-9818482-6-6